Copyright ©G:
ISBN 978-1-8:
A Salt Swan P

DEAD POETS PEN

Dead Poets Pen is the true story of something quite extraordinary that happened to me in 1994. Whilst sitting at home I felt an overwhelming need to write. I wasn't one who wrote in general, so this was something out of the ordinary. I took a pen and paper from the draw and suddenly began to write. The words written on the paper were not my own thoughts but were coming from some extraneous source. After a couple of minutes of writing at speed, without punctuation or any grammar I found before me over 260 words. On reading was written it appeared someone was talking to me. After telling a friend about this remarkable happening he asked if I could write in front of him and this I did (the full story is in my book 'In Search of the Swan'). To his and my astonishment exactly the same thing happened and 200 words or so later, again written at great speed and without grammar or punctuation words flowed through me from this extraneous source. On reading it to him I discovered his wife had a doctor's appointment the previous day. There was no way possible I could have known this fact. We were both totally shocked when he revealed that his wife did indeed have an appointment with her doctor the previous day. So shocked was my friend by this that I never saw him for about ten years after. For me it was the start of something truly astonishing. This was to me something truly unexplainable to a logical and rational mind but every time I picked up a pen and paper I could write at will the thoughts from this extraneous source. I was given past, present and future insight which proved accurate.

One day some three months after the initial event happening I began to hear the words I would write. It was not only conversational text but profound philosophy; this was then followed by poetry. The contents of this book contain those written pieces that have come throughout the following years. I have given all the pieces a title and added to the best of my ability the grammar and punctuation. The words are as I thought I heard them and may or may not be totally correct in every single case, but near as damn it. I have included four of the original written pieces at the beginning of the book for the reader to fully comprehend how the poetry first appeared to me in written form. As time progressed many pieces were written on a computer in the first instance and therefore there are no original writings as such. However the originals on paper I do have stand testimony to my story.

 The works contain many differing subjects such as love, the mind, beauty and war as well as other various pieces and aspects of nature and life. The personalities in the pieces and their style would lead you to believe they are not from the same person but from a number of people. I myself was from the East End of London and I had a very limited education leaving school at 15. What I find incredible is not only were they all written at great speed, with no grammar or punctuation and making perfect sense but they were given to me from start to finish in one go, taking under two minutes to write in most cases. I was dictated the pieces by someone I couldn't see, smell or touch and could only hear them in the confines of mind, in what I can only describe as a thought voice with words given to me to transcribe onto the paper. Quite how it all happens that is the great mystery. I will leave the reader to ponder the pieces and come to their own conclusion.

Science tells us the mind is part of the brain and it is an accepted view. In my humble opinion in over 25 years of writing from an extraneous source it has taught me this is impossible, and here is why: On death the brain dies and with it mind, well that is the accepted view, but what about my writings and communication from the extraneous source? This clearly shows various minds at work, using me as a vessel for their thoughts, poetry, philosophy, future predictions, communication, insight etc. What the enormous volume of works show you are that death has not meant the death of mind, on the contrary, I believe mind survives death, meaning it cannot possibly be part of the brain as we believe but a separate entity. The mind to me is the soul and the soul the muse. If you believe the soul exists as I know for certain it does, then our understanding of mind and what we are taught simply cannot be right! I have had people say I have a multi personality disorder, that it all comes from my own mind etc but the reality is I have seen the future before it happened and have written about things I could never have known about. The tansy fly for example in one of the poems was made extinct in the last century and there was no way possible I could have heard of that. How much is from my own mind who truly knows? What we can be certain of is that the extraneous source has provided me with a stream of endless material and today still does. I believe 'Dead Poets Pen' aptly describes the book.

Example 1

No time when I do sleep

v

Example 2
Beautiful sight

If thou art not More
beauteous then that of
a 1,000 Suns or a 1,000
Stars then blind are
If thou art less beautiful
If the Heavens above
then the Painters thought
a the Painters Vision
then Most My Vision
deemed failed sight
If beauty been delightful
Muse the Scorns at
Jealous eyes do cast
and yet do Please and
delight my vision the
beautiful beautiful sight
My beauty of eye and
Mind   written 7 June 96

VI

Example 3

Despairing conscience

My despairing Conscience torn in two evading truth and finding Irrelevance a Sordid friend Perpetual deviance Soiling a mind weakened Pitied am I to chose between a Conscience Soiled and truth pervades me a tolerance or Persuing a mind of indifference Perceive in minds eye a tolerate side a Conscience to truck but woe is me tis time of Madness Melancoly me and a Conscience Soiled.

13 Jan 95.

VII

Example 4

Lost in the winds that blow

Though young am I
and fortunes fade so
quickly his honor, His day
I lay fallen with,
friends, barely knew
Such is this war
Oh lovely war where
numbers nor names have
meaning. Dreams lay
scattered in fields with
fires burning into the night
wretched war that cursed
war what scars the heart
Beneath a soldiers lie in
a wanton war corpse from
the bloody fields where
have reason the hope

VIII

Index

Beauty

1. Beauty
2. Forever its beauty send
3. Beautiful by memory
4. Age
5. The looking glass
6. A face of such beauty
7. Hideous face
8. A painter's eye
9. Beautiful sight
10. Time's dial
11. Beauty I eyed this day
12. On canvas lay perfection

Various

13. Ode to Shakespeare
14. Gentle I
15. A painting of life
16. John Keats
17. Rupert Brooke
18. Poets delight

19. A letter to Marilyn Monroe
20. Life and death
21. Pen and muse
22. The Gambler
23. Words I write
24. One's own self
25. The Artist
26. Seven ages
27. The human being
28. Ashes of dreams
29. I am
30. Times dial
31. Time
32. No time
33. Life
34. Our England
35. Ode to Sir Francis Bacon

Love

36. The perfect love
37. You and I
38. Lovers by the seaside
39. One day
40. Now you're not there
41. My friend and lover
42. The sweetest of fragrance

43. My hell
44. Dangerous liaisons
45. My artist friend
46. Just at this time
47. Rapturous love
48. To Reason love and what it is?
49. Not in love
50. If I could have told you
51. Love's richness
52. I so lucky in love
53. A place for lovers
54. Only me that she thinks
55. She is but nine
56. Man with a desire for man
57. I knew what love was

Nature
58. Daffodils
59. Astronomy speaks
60. Dream of past
61. Winter woe
62. Summers day
63. Pleasure to seek
64. Crocus bulbs and tansy fly
65. Heavenly moon
66. Magical night of stars that fall

67. Hark thee oh bird
68. The riverbank
69. Appear unto me
70. Oh to be a bird
71. Magic of night
72. Night of most beauteous sky
73. The crested lark
74. Heavenly sun
75. Heaven's door
76. Papa meilland

Mind

77. Silent whisper
78. I and me
79. Divide of man and mind
80. Upon an hill
81. Yesterday's dream
82. Conscience
83. Despairing conscience
84. The beauty of mind
85. Conscience beyond repair
86. Beauty of mind
87. The astronomers mind
88. Mind and youth
89. Poem on dementia – The I once was

War

90. The Poppy

91. Lost in the winds that blow

92. Weep for me

93. Land or riches

94. If I were a soldier

95. Could I do it?

96. Soldier brave

97. Cemetery of war

98. Etched in some memory

Death

99. Sleep like death

100. Here lay truth

101. My friend death

102. One hour mine

103. Death do tell

104. The petals of a rose

105. On death

106. A pillow of tears – mourning a mother – The Cockney Bard

BEAUTY

Beauty

Beauty never fades, nor does the sun extinguish its
Fire. For what is beauty? If you say I know, you'd be
A liar. Beauty to one is not to another. To a mirror it
Is all things and nothing. Beauty is a perfection,
Unblemished and undefined. It is a pleasure
Unrestrained to the eye. To one beauty can be a rose
In full bloom and to another the seed in the palm of
His hand. In the darkness beauty is but a moment in
The mind, and in the light, it is a perception of one's
Own judgement. Beauty you are an illusion, a
Deception, a fool's gold. All things to all men. In
Revealing her I too am condemned to the fickle folly
Of describing beauty!

Forever its beauty send

Did ever more beauty speak words, than eyes
Touched by heavenly spheres, where beauties eyes
Did gaze their most important deeds. Were ever
More beauty to descend from creative imagery,
Where pictures of mind do cast a visionary sight,
Enfolding dreams of night. Stars and moon, sun and
Air do share your beauty and if perchance thy vision
End, thy mind forever its beauty send.

Beautiful by memory

Compare thee to beauty once was, a picture no
Longer seen. Compare thee to the maiden fair who
Lost her looks, frail and haggard thus is. Compare
Thee to the memory of sun filled day but now 'tis
Winter's show of savagery. The withered rose lay
Pitied, fallen on winter's day. No more to shine
Gloriously. No more to bring beauty to mine eyes.
Oh rose, I remember thou beauty on summer's day.
I remember thee that way. Beauteous and adored.
Withered by eye, but beautiful by memory.

Age

Age methinks doth enhance my beauty, embracing a
Mind of youth once was, with wisdom now seen and
Enjoyed. Methinks beauty thus sweeter with age, and
Desire I not for past. And yet, where youth once did
Lay a tender head, 'tis now but a mellowed dream.
Methinks how beautiful life, how wondrous age, and
The passing of time doth please. Never I to shed but
A tear, yet love each hour, each day, each year, and
Beauty surround me. 'Tis I whom eye the beauty of
Age and life.

The looking glass

The glass upon beauties wasted youth spent, thus a
Vanity to assume a conscience of despairing
Persuasion. A beauty bear no ill. Thou looking glass
Now can tell how beauty wear with time. Pitiful
Time, that set the maiden fair unconquering task of
Beauty kept. 'Tis glass forewarning of perils seen.
Future comes and skin so fair, becomes pale and
Drawn and beauties gone!

A face of such beauty

Were ever your beauty to smile, 'tis more the sanity
Of mind deceived and yet were ever to please a face
Of such beauty. Were ever more beauty to touch and
Grace, so sweet a charmed face, where heaven did
Smile before thee in celebrated glee. Oh see with
Eyes whom whisper silent verse, a magical spell,
Never to seek or tell a beauty's tale. Fortunes bless
Thy skin so fair and words the poet speak so well,
Voice thy beauty's fallible hell. Never thus to shame
The rose but thus he did compare. 'Twas beauty
Bound upon thy lips that ever more a pleasure
Shared, than eyes did ever see such beauty. I know
Nothing of the rules of poetry but I do know the
Language of love, inspiration and the fires of muse
In which my soul thrives.

Hideous face

My friend pray tell of thy hideous face upon which
Turns me ill, and yet once there was such beauty. A
Man whom I pray tell did love and yet do scorn thee
Now. For thou art hideous and I no longer regard
Thee with affection befitting of love. 'Tis noble of
Thee to intrude this day and I deem thou a friend
But lover no more. Doth the blade who cut so sharp
Render thee a quivering fool? Speak thy fine fellow
Once was. Be told a story of brave heart and courage
And perchance thou hideous face will seem but fine.
Ah but 'tis foolish to assume thy face of which
Grotesquely offends could once more be beautiful to
My vision. Pray tell my lover once was, but alas are
No more. Take thee away and allow my memory a
Subject of good thoughts.

The painter's friend

If not but a painters frown doth please the eye.
Wer't not a description of incandescent light? Do
Brush the living image from thou sight. To paint
Such beauty before night doth end. And yet, the
Mind a painter's friend, do send a vision unseen and
The conscience wills such misery. For in one
Moment of pretence the image forever beauty reign,
Painters sight a replenished view, where beauty now
Perceived. And yet, the image of conscience matters
The will and sends thee to hell in visionary sight. To
Be of beauty once painting done, and then beauty
Becomes the painter's friend.

Beautiful sight

If thou art more beautiful than that of a thousand
Suns or a thousand stars, then blind am I. If thou
Art less beautiful than the heavens above, or the
Painters thought, then most my vision deemed
Failed sight. If beauty bear delightful muse, the
Scorns of jealous eye do cast, and yet do please and
Delight my vision. This beautiful, beautiful sight.
My beauty of eye and mind.

Times dial

Her beauty not lost by times dial. Her age, ageless.
For beauty captured in mind's eye. Time the taker
Of beauty so thou art feared. Yet time thou can
Never take away the image of beauty from me. Who
Art thou time with hours that do run so fast and
Leave despairing beauty. Yet through mind it can
Never be taken. Though time does clutch the hand
So fair, never in mine eyes 'tis lost. Beckon thee
Forth time to cease, thus beauty never ends.
Eternally youthful her skin soft and gentle. Time and
Beauty hand in hand stilled. And yet if mind doth
See time then beauty will be gone through days
Hours. Beauty is blessed in eye of mind and beauty
Forever stayed, thus time ticks irrelevant.

Beauty I eyed this day

'Tis perfection that I did eye this day. A perfection
Compared to beauty unblemished. A perfection
That caress the soul and sweet nature could only
Dream but of being equal. 'Tis hair raven black and
Eyes that do smile a thousand smiles, skin like silk.
A finer face could not have been woven by God's
Own weaver. 'Tis beauty I eyed this day.

On canvas lay perfection

Methinks her beauty 'tis but a sun whom shine and a
Moon whom whisper the soft soothing melodies of
Love. Where arrows of love did aspire and delight
Me. Beauteous maiden whose lips I hath taste, never
To forget such succulence. Soft, gentle skin do I
Embrace, thy sweet, sweet face. If ever love did
Entomb my conscience, 'tis your beauty still. My
Hand doth see the painters hand to beautify thee.

On canvas lay perfection. Speak words describing
Beauty, thus if ever the mind deceive and beauty
Wer't gone, such treachery befall me. For thou art
Beauty and beauty art thou. A passion stills my
Pounding heart and fires they burn this night,
Brighter than the sun, sweet sun. Thou art most
Beauteous and thou art mine. Each breath I thee
Breathe taste of thou, and ever will mine love be
Yours.

VARIOUS

Ode to Shakespeare

I am a pen of many minds, but who can guess which
Ones to find? Marlowes, Jonsons, Bacons bee,
Oxford, Lord Strange, maybe Dee? Not the Doctor,
This can't be! I don't believe he wrote did he? What
Of Raleigh, what a pen, words, words, words his one
True friend. Secret codes so true concealed, surely
Now to be revealed? School of night I hear you cry,
Walsingham he was a spy. You haven't mentioned
Good Queen Bess, ah the virgin – you must jest.
Some say Fletcher, Beaumont's key, and Hilliard to
Paint that tree. So very small he must make it fit. A
Face to paint, but what mind was it? Florio's first
Fruits did he taste. Daniel, Donne and Spenser not
Forgot in haste. A mighty pen, pure genius they say,
For it has caused so much dismay. Hoffman, Dodd
And many more have searched to find this man for
Sure. But who, oh who can the great man be?
William Shakespeare I honour thee!

Gentle I

I gentle as a summer's day, fiercer than the autumn
Winds, colder than the hearts delay. I gentle as a
Morn in May, as the spring is sprung, as the lambs
First breath. The ghost of death shall pass me by, the
Darkest night and the tear of eye. Shadows fade into
The night, the crisp frost dew upon the leaf, the quill
Before me writes. I as gentle as the night, as still as
The bird in flight, when the arrow renders life no
More. Be as I not as before, gentle as a summer's
Day.

A painting of life

I painted the picture of life. I used images in my
Mind. I used colours to portray emotion. I used
Strokes that move in time with the days of life. I
Used mirrors that reflect the image in the face of the
Tired man. I used conundrums to fill the minds of
Those whom search the painting. I used degrees of
Self to portray my picture. The picture, a painting of
Life.

John Keats

How when someone speaks of your name a flawless
Image does spring to mind. And yet, you Keats,
Shunned by a world for your dulcet tones can move
The soul in ways few can ever do. Your words taken
From a mind so pure, it dignifies indifference. In
You Keats is that nightingale which sings its sweet
Melody. I too can feel in you the pain, the agony of a
Poet lost. Neither words, nor actions can fall foul of
The greatness bestowed upon you, but among others
Who deem you worthless. Only death could bring
You respect among peers. Laid to rest so young and
Yet so wise. It is in tribute I write my words to a
Fellow Cockney poet and raise a glass to Mr Keats.

Rupert Brooke

In some ways the whole point of your poetical
Existence was missed. How glory came in the lines
Of just one poem 'The Soldier' when in so many
Others, death and its meaning, seem lost and
Pointless. The flames of passion that left your pen
Are a reminder to all, of the joys a poet can bring.
No wasted words or sentiments, no ideal spanning
Mind, fruitless in its endeavours, but an eternal
Mind, able to seek and find, whatever it so seeks. I
Speak like you from the same mind. Your death, a
Sacrifice laid in a foreign field. Not battle or wound
But ill health took a light from you in life. Now it
Shines hereafter in death in people's hearts and
Minds.

A poet's delight

The willing of thy wit, the laughter held within, the
Poet's word so sweetly aired, a justice in my song.
Patience precludes me a selfish denial but last not
My feelings insecure, alas my woe in words. A valued
Antiquity of books, whom briefly held a muse in
Mind, judge not I or seem to find, words to please
Me. Insincere me, but words of wit I write, a poet's
Delight, a muse of deep denial. Hearty and wise, a
Wisdom foreseen in books of old that seem to tell
What has been, will be, and thy future come. Pray
Thee well thy poets mind.

A letter to Marilyn Monroe

Who could have ever dreamed of the life you would
Have. A babe to a beauty, unknown to an idol. Who
Truly knew you, the Hollywood star? Who could
Have loved you more than the millions now? I think
I kind of knew you, somewhere in my distant past, a
Girl with a head full of dreams. Where love deserted
You, hope never did. Where pain tortured and
Racked you, hope never did. Where too many judged
You, without care or remorse. Marilyn Monroe, we
Knew only a shadow of what you were. Tears wore
Like a mask where only your smile could deceive. I
Think that I love you now. I think that I loved you
Then. Love, sweet Marilyn, that was you. You were
So funny and bright too. Not at all dizzy, oh no, not
You! Beauty personified. Man's perfect dream. No
One could doubt you were a star in all scenes. All
That we are left with is all that you were. Love,
Beauty and a star in an uncaring world.

Life & Death, a human adventure

Although my life is soon to end I ponder mistakes I
Have made. I grieve for a life wasted in short spans,
For my time callous in places. Who am I, what am I
On a road I briefly touched. I endeavored to be the
Best I could, when I could, but learning for me was a
Barrage of obtrusive sentiments, blocking an
Otherwise sensitive human being. I hated me at
Times with such a despairing loathing of who I
Should be, what I should be. In truth life seemed to
Pass me by. So here I am facing death, a certainty.
Its revelation soon thrust upon me. I know not of
Death & what I shall face. I love to imagine it is
Some wonderful paradise, where many before me
Have walked, and where many will do so after my
Demise. I want to imagine many will celebrate my
Passing, but in reality I know no paradise, and no
Joyous celebration of the life I have had.

What will become of me as death knocks at my
Door? No celebration, no light, no darkness,
Nothing? I am to believe that? My all, my everything
Comes down to one moment in a lifetime, when I
Close my eyes for a final time, perhaps scanning a
Lifetime of memories? Perhaps an empty void where
They should be? I realise now as death calls me that
Life could have be kinder, I could have been better,
But my lasting memory was how short it all was, and
That nothing could have prepared me for death.

Death, be nice to me, be painless, be ruthless &
Quick for you are all I have left. I cannot foresee
Tomorrow. My needs are few, my wants are many
But life & death are part of my journey, your journey
Too! Say goodbye from me won't you as I sail on my
Merry way. Raise a glass or tip your hat. Please don't
Forget me as life surely will. Death will embrace me,
Will comfort me, will bring me all I never found.
And who knows I may return a better man on the
Road we know as life.

Pen and muse

Methods madness thee I grasp. Bared a soul of Irrevocable need, yet persuade my eye of beautiful Bond. The poet's words so tender, need filled my Brow of comfort's seed. Words thy wit, forthwith do Ride. Playing words of gracious intent, beautiful and Meant to ease thy mind on summer's day. Summer's Sun doth shine and my quill doth ease of beautiful Words, ah such beautiful words. Thus my life Fulfilled, yet puzzled my will. 'Tis glory of pen and Muse.

The Gambler

Oh the life of the gambler. He, whose dreams are
Raised and crushed. Who has the world before him
And yet, can feel the world against him. In the head
Of a horse, or the turn of a card, can be rich or
Ruined. Oh the life of the gambler. The exit door
Tells him no more and yet more dreams will come
Tomorrow. The pain, the joy, the thrill, the drama
But oh the cost can be so much more, than pennies
Or pounds. No one sees the devastation as the
Turmoiled mind seeks solace. But brave or foolish
He may well be, stupid, even naive to believe, but
Believe he must, for dreams to come true. Don't tell
The gambler you never win and that the road is a
Fruitless hell. The door going in represents a world
Of opportunity, the door going out represents lost
And shattered dreams. Today's loss, tomorrow's
Gain, be lucky my friend. Oh the life of the gambler.

Words I write

Do I a man so proud and so full share in my
Thoughts with my work. I write on some paper the
Meaning of life and these to the people are taught.
My inner most feelings are shared with you all, the
Deepness of words that I write. I share my words
With the world outside, with the world I share my
Thoughts. I also share my heart, and if
Understanding is thrust upon you through my work,
My words are all worthwhile.

One's own face

Times of solitude, thus to breathe in the air of sweet
Justice. To weep thy tears of waters rain.
To assemble thy lucid paramount of lives obstacle.
To act on thy insolvent duty of sceptical annulment
Ridiculing a personal crusade of melted conscience,
Whereby thy mind seeps its judgment of reality,
Upon endless, endless meandering. Wasted pieces of
Life's short span. Cursed life on day of death that
Weeps tears upon thy soul. At peace thy body, at
Peace with natures green, flowers, wind that pass
You by. A caricature of a famous poet lay upon the
Desk. An empty, empty drawing of which gives the
Impression life. It seems safe to assume a majestic
Conscience of matter, to thus be afraid of one's own
Face.

The Artist - Dante Gabriel Rossetti

I am as art but a mere canvas upon which every
Thought is detailed and given substance. The
Colours excel in my desire to fulfill my dream of a
Painting that defines what I am as a man. The brush
Moves like a ballerina in graceful pursuit of the
Perfect dance. I can be forgiven my weariness at
Times, when the day's long, long hours play mischief
With my mind. A reluctance to sleep that weary head
Buried in an object desire for perfection, where my
Soul can delight in a pleasure to all senses, but in
Particular the pleasure of eye and mind. As an artist I
Am reminded throughout my life of the pain such
Perfection can bring. With brush and palette I
Require far more than just good thoughts to enjoy
My day. I require patience personified, a stillness of
Hand, and a beautifying deliberation of my soul to
Greet the dawn with the finished piece.

Seven ages

The baby, the age of which innocence begins its first
Breath. The Infant, the age of love unconditional
And true. The child, the age where the ideas of
Fantasy flourish. The teen, the age of the world of
Discovery. The adult, the age of the world of harsh
Reality. The old, the age of wisdom and sometimes
Regret. The death, the age where all become equal.

The human being

Oh the human being, that complex character.
Unfathomable, unpredictable, human being.
Who in their head goes, where no one knows.
Silly, emotional, brave at times, utterly stupid at
Times human being. who toils, sometimes in deceit,
To achieve their day. I often wonder on observing
This rather strange character, if I am alone in
Understanding the immense diversity of substance
From one to the other. From the utterly sublime to
The ridiculous. I am left to wonder if life and nature
Has less surprises than mankind. I know you human
Being, I truly do. No, in fact human being, I don't
Know you at all!

Ashes of dreams

The trials and tribulations of a human being. The
Exhaustion and exuberation of pulling defeat from
The flames of fire. The pain, the anguish of loss, the
Barren self, the drive and enthusiasm to be all that
You can. The fickle hours, those endless hours to
Achieve a goal. Running with ecstasy, falling with
Optimisms flawed dream. The hope filled challenge
Of the Olympian to achieve first prize, becoming
God like in a supreme test of will, determination and
Courage, challenging the body and spirit to reach
Unprecedented heights. The exhausted, elated, pain
Ridden, defeated, deflated, emotional being the
Athlete. Driven by their quest to succeed in a search
For perfection. Resurrecting the eternal flame from
The ashes of dreams.

I am

I am in all things and nothing. I am the winds that
Blow. I am the raging seas that calm and the drops
Of rain that fall. I am the life in all forms, the sun,
Moon, stars and the air. I am the birds that sing and
All that it brings, I am, that I am, that I am. I am the
Mountains, the streams, the brooks and the dales,
The tears of a child and the smile of the knave. The
Widow weeps, the grave sits bare, for where once
Life was, no longer there. I am your dreams, your
Nightmares too. I am the wise and the stupid fool.
I am not once or thrice divine. I am not more or less
Defined. I am all things and nothing that is what I
Am.

Times dial

Her beauty not lost by times dial. Her age, ageless.
For beauty captured in mind's eye. Time the taker of
Beauty so thou art feared. Yet time thou can never
Take away the image of beauty from me. Who art
Thou time with hours that do run so fast and leave
Despairing beauty. Yet through mind it can never be
Taken. Though time does clutch the hand so fair,
Never in mine eyes 'tis lost. Beckon thee forth time
To cease, thus beauty never ends. Eternally youthful
Her skin soft and gentle. Time and beauty hand in
Hand stilled. And yet if mind doth see time then
Beauty will be gone through day's hours. Beauty is
Blessed in eye of mind and beauty forever stayed,
Thus time ticks irrelevant.

Time

When as time began to slide I look at an eternity
Beyond the grave. You have time that ticks so
Slowly, without time are we. You have time that
Takes you day to day, we have no time. Let the
Clocks and watches tell the time no more. For
Eternity, it has no time, no time and that's for sure.

No time when I do sleep

Methinks time the dial of day speak words of
Irrelevance, words of disdain. Inappropriate words,
Ill words on this day, a day of despair. My
Conscience play a sombre tune of which I sigh this
Day, I crie a tear that fall. Sadly longing, despised
Each word that describes time. Methinks day must
Turn to night for sigh to turn to sleep, to dream
Forgetting time and day. No more disdain, my
Pleasure gained for sleep becomes my friend. Words
Of ill no longer heard as I do gentle sleep. Silent
Night, my conscience rest and freed my plight. My
Cursed mind no more to rage, no time when I do
Sleep.

Life

Life thou art the giver, but thou art the taker of this
Breath that I breathe. Thou art the morning sun and
My night time moon. Thou art the messenger of
Good tidings and woe. Thou art the wise man and
The fool. Thou art the saint and the sinner and thou
Art the cathedral and the teller of tales, to which I
Assume a debt of gracious thanks. But thee oh life,
Cause me such pain and who render me at times less
Than a man, whose word is hereby lost among those
With deafened ears. And yet like the statue whose
Erect torso stands proud, can give to the multitude a
Sense of celebration and fulfillment. Oh life, spare
Me the Injustice of awaking my inner sanctimonious
Heart but fill me with the joyous spring of
Knowledge, wherein my cup shall runneth over in
The well heeled justice of the good and well
Meaning. For life must be my patience, my wisdom
And my clarity, of which I breathe a love and
Equality of all mankind.

Our England

England, our beautiful, bountiful land. Unsurpassed
In all its beauty. Abundant in all its pleasures. What
The eye doth see no artist could truly paint. My
Beautiful, bountiful, fertile England. What doth thou
Say oh envious nations whom cast with jealous eye
The crown in natures glory? Rich beyond compare is
He whom breathes this English air. Oh to be born
Of this glorious isle. The rose we call our England.

Ode to Sir Francis Bacon

Good Queen Bess she had a lover
Robert Dudley she did smother.
She did take him to her bed.
And those in Spain say she is wed!
Goodness me a Virgin Queen.
A secret kept away unseen.
Her Spanish suitor called a halt
To the desire he had brought.
But that's not all for there is more,
She had a child and that's for sure.

A royal child but never king,
And on her finger she wore no ring.
I jest you not this very day,
I tell you where the king doth lay.
Pray tell, not where it is said,
For in that place he lay not dead.
A picture gives the game away,
For royalty in this display.

A Touchstone, a Solomon here on earth.
A tribute to show him for all his worth.
His body is buried obscurely
And now it's discovered so surely.
Consumed with delight, we give honour to thee,
Who layeth not in Saint Albans but Saint Gregorys.

LOVE

The perfect love

I am looking and searching for heartfelt happiness.

I look and I seek to find, what in all essence
Something that doesn't even exist is perhaps, I
Search the depths of my heart for reason but the
Reason is no longer there. In searching for this
Wonderful love I miss so many opportunities to
Broaden my horizons, but I know its there, it must
Be there, for I cannot settle for anything less than
The perfect love.

You and I

You and I had a dream, you and I could see forever,
You and I. Now I is all that's left. I miss the nights
Of togetherness. I miss the angry exchanges when I
Was right and you were wrong! What the heck! I
Miss the walks, the days out, the fun, the gaiety. I
Sure as hell miss you. I know despite the passing of
Time I would not have changed you for the world,
For I loved you then and I still love you now, the
Days of you and I. I wonder where you are now. I
Suppose you're happy? But in my sadness the pain
That runs deep is eased only by your memory. I feel
So lost at times. I know the you and I should still be
There, but now there is only I.

Lovers by the seaside

Scurrying along I gave the pebbles in me pocket to
Margaret, ooh, we are in love. The pebbles collected
From the beach in Brighton. Ooh, how I love the
Day at the seaside. Full of sun, fun, the paddle in the
Sea, ice cream and candy floss, ooh, how I enjoyed
Me day. Margaret is only young but as sweet as a
Rose. She has the heart of an angel and I do love her
So. Margaret and I plan to wed. Ooh, I just can't
Wait for the day. Just think me married, whatever
Next! Lovers by the seaside. Ooh, my idea of bliss!
Stealing a kiss from under her kiss me quick hat. Roll
On next year for our summer fun to begin again, but
Next time I'll be married. Cheerio.

One day in your life

Given a day in your life I would choose the day we
Met, ooh, how I enjoyed that day. I still remember as
The rain came down, how your little face cringed. I
Do remember so how your hair swept unkempt. It
Rather bemused me to see you rain sodden, against a
Backdrop of houses covered in grime and dirt filled
Bags. Ooh, you did look lovely! I remember you
Having smiled and that distinctive cheeky grin. Ooh,
How I remember that day. I often think of that first
Kiss and dream of you that way. Oh give me this
Please I say.

Now you're not there

Smiling through the tears of a broken heart, lost in a
World of darkness, the light removed. When love
Was gone given no reason. So lost in a pool of
Sentiment. Struggling to capture the essence of my
Imagination about love and the way it feels. How
When in love it feels so good but when love is gone,
Oh how it hurts. The shambolic nature of happiness.
How my heart does cry its song of sadness, now love
Is not here.

My friend and lover

Succumb to sweet temptation, where lips succulent
Did I embrace, to taste but fair. Thou doth render
Me captivated, and I assume pity for the man who
Taste not my delight. Heaven and the heavenly
Spheres hath captured thy beauty, to bless me this
Morn and breathed the fires of passion before me.
Moon, stars and the glorious sun seduce my
Thoughts and tempt province this day. O maiden,
Thou art a painting, whose artist did spend but days
Perfecting. A beauty that shines like rays of sunlight
Through clouds of white and 'tis I who wish my love
Forever twined in harmonious rapture. Pray tell my
Judgement true, and thou art the love of all loves,
And in my wisdom proclaim a love more beautiful
Than the angels kiss. To taste so sweet, your lips I
Choose above all other, my friend and lover.

The Sweetest of fragrance

Ah love the sweetest of all fragrance I hath taste.
Such delight that my heart, whom in times of joy
Portray the desperation of a rabbit, whom fear for its
Very existence. Such is my love at this time the
World is before me and the heavens are my best
Friend, to whom the world spins on its axis, an
Excitement of merry. Indeed I feel congratulating
My sincerity in abundance, bloom the sweet rose to
Which my fondness be known. Such exuberance
Pertaining delight. 'Tis I, who in callous
Abandonment, risk my all in pursuit of a maiden fair.
But 'tis stupendous and delicious my thoughts of
Mind, who scourers the depths seeking comfort. In
My imagination such turgid thoughts running like
The spring lamb in gay abundance, whispering silent
The love I know. Perchance a sight of love's tender
Explanation, delivered unto me in such richness.
Forsake not the memory of love, but flow the
Thoughts of morning when my arms are filled with
Thee.

My hell

My sweet conscience embarking a twisted denial.
A solitude of incoherent knowledge, assembled
Hastily. Bickering impatiently, words that cry a
Sadness within. A plenitude of misery placed upon
My heart. Ah my heart, but a beating coil that love
Did tempt. Pursued I, a lonely road of which hell
Became my friend, a friend of woe. Love, the
Sweetest of God's deliverance and yet, mine heart is
But a weeping stream, where love did taste so sweet,
And yet did poison. My dreams did follow me and
Haunt me still, and my love from whence my dream
Did come, vacates my heart and torments my mind,
That cursed love. Embrace the fantasy of love's
Foreboding dream, for which no man dare taste its
Wickedness. 'Twas I who did seek the solace of a
Love, but found my hell.

Dangerous liaisons

Dangerous liaisons, stolen passion, creeping like a
Cat to the boudoir of a lady. I steal my moments
When I can, for if I am caught execution awaits but I
Cannot resist my sweet lady. Her heart is full of love,
Alas our love can never be and my heart aches for
My lady. I ponder on the night before and eagerly
Await my next conquest. I love her sweet charms
And to be wrapped in her arms is just heavenly.
How could anyone resist such temptation? I throw
Caution to the wind in search of my bliss and that
Dangerous kiss from my dangerous

My artist friend

Love so rich, assuming a love of toiled intent.
Oh love whom know, abandon not. I see you in my
Heart, a configuration of finesse, awakening my
Brow of happiness. Be I of knowledge, irrational
Knowledge, quivering in mind to thus perpetrate a
Deluge of wistful woe. Belonging and ignoring
Feelings of heart. Oh pretend, Oh pretend, of love
What I see. Pretend knowingly assuming joy. Piffle
Thy mind of squalid intent; of love I know nay more
Than loosely fitting canvas to thus arouse my artist
Friend. Do I depict a jealous eye to spy upon my
Love so rare? Emotions raised, fallen skies, lifeless
Image of love that scars. mortal wound, an arrows
Pent, vengeance, martyr, why oh why? The fated
Image of love perceives, deceives, my artist's friend,
Love.

Just at this time

The skies so clear and blue, the brook it winds along
The dale. The subtle breeze blows gently and
Passion fills my heart, but I am given my first lesson
Of sweet and tender love. How the skies seem far
Away as I lay and gaze aghast. My fair lady I dream
Like you of the days to come for us. Frightened
Rabbits scurry as movement comes from afar, but
Peace and calm do return as I hold you in my arms.
Leave me never my fair maiden, for I do love you so.
I am to lay my head right down, and drift into a flow
Of thoughts and images stretching my mind, how
Joyous my life is just at this time.

Rapturous love

'Twere a love so rich. A love to splendour my heart. A love too fickle by far and yet fortuitous I to Embrace the arms of such beauty. Thou art before Me like the sun and the heavens, creating bliss, a Night time kiss, I celebrate thee. The magical Heavens thee I ask to sing unto me and serenade my Good fortune. Alas I seek not of your knowledge or Wisdom of words, but a blessing upon me. Desire Me, desire my muse, for thou art bliss my love I kiss So oft poor lips are raw. Too wish my heart such Succulent feast. A love too taste forever. Rapturous Love embrace me till I breathe nay more.

To reason love and what it is

Loss brings so much pain. Who has never suffered
Loss? Who has never felt pain? Each day brings a
Memory, a thought, a tear. Embracing love of which
Is life's essence, brings with it life's great despair,
When that which was once solid becomes thin air.
Regrets frequent an otherwise sane mind. I should
Have done this or not done that. I believe in love
More than anything this God damn life has to offer.
Love of life, love of another human being. In a
Human's capacity to think deeply on matters
Regarding the heart, one is to compound the
Simplicity of love into a far deeper semblance of
Reality than need be. I love and need to be loved.
One needs not to think too deeply on this. To love
Once or a million times is not to understand love.
Love has no limits, no boundaries, no magic
Formula.

Not in love

Not in love, merely captivated by your presence, and
Intoxicated by a beauty that has no equal. Love my
Spoil the image I now see, but if given my chance I
Would surely love you.

If I could have told you

If I could have told you, I would have told you, but I
Couldn't tell you, no way. I tried hard to tell you, I
Wanted to tell you, but I couldn't tell you, no way. In
Heart rending pleas, I searched on my knees, for
Answers, for ways to tell you, but I couldn't tell you,
I swear I couldn't tell you, and now you have gone
Away. And I only wanted to tell you, I loved you.

Love's richness

'Twas summer's sun and winter's fall that love did
Bloom. The perpetual sweetness of her voice thus
Melodious tones of harmonious music, played so
Sweetly, softly, gently upon mine ears. Love the
Creative genius of cupid, whose arrow in flight did
Render me captivated. Thou art my perfection of
Mind. such beauty enriching my vision. Ah there,
Love's richness.

I so lucky in love

Beauteous maiden I do love thee. Thou art all my
Desires and wishes fulfilled. A subservient of my
Imagination to whom fruitful desire fill up my heart.
If but in my dreams my beauteous maiden did aspire
To delight me, then dream I may and not delay. My
Laws contempt a pining soul, whose perfection is
But life itself. And yet what beauty my eyes do
Perceive. So beauteous, wherefore my heart doth
Pound like hooves of horses in battle. Such delight
To mind. Be I so kind as to presume my desire for
Thee? Thou art my maiden so fair and I so lucky in
Love.

A place for lovers

January in Paris,
Eros speaks of love.
Sensual, magical
Under a starlit sky.
In Paris Painters & Poets delight,
Sun awaits the early morn.
Carefree lovers steal a kiss,
Holding hands along the seine,
All so beautiful, serene this night.
Romantic, erotic, pure pieces of time.
Life is simply perfect here
In Paris, wonderful Paris.
Evermore, a place of such exquisite love & beauty.

Only me that she thinks

Erupting pleasure as my naked body becomes rigid.
With pleasure my naked body tingles. With desire
Her body so tempting. With curves that roll and dip
It seems forever. With her vivacious personality and
Heavenly face, her love for me seems endless, but I
Often wonder is it with me that this love takes place
Or does she dream of another? I feel at a loss
Sometimes to try and discover such an answer but I
Fear her reply and I believe it is not in my interest to
Know, so I choose to remain silent. In trusting her I
Forgive my thoughts but the pleasure I do give is
Doubled, if I am convinced it is with me only that
She thinks.

She is but nine

Dangerous feelings of emotional bliss that torment
My very soul. I placate from my desire for someone
Less than a women. In devilment my heart it does
Flutter but merely for a child. It cannot be right that
I am in love with someone so young, but my feelings
Do come from sympathy and not indulgence. But I
Have been given to thinking had time not been so
Cruel, for I am but seventy and she is but nine.

Man with a desire for man

I look upon you as an object of my desire, strong,
Virile man. Carved is your body like a Greek God.
A beauty normally confined to the features of a
Woman. In my inner most sanctum are doubts about
Who I should be, what I should be, but I doubt not
The love I have for you, man carved of stone. In a
Pleasurable desire to thought and mind, I think long
And hard about you, but to some I am misguided
And wrong. Within me love burns and my heart
Aches. Who is anybody to judge me? A man with a
Desire for man.

I knew what love was

When all the winds have calmed. The sea waves
Crash against the shore no more. The sun flickers
Its light against the dying embers of a man's last
breath. I shall remember only one thing, I love, was
Loved and knew what love was.

NATURE

Daffodils

How I do love the flowers. Golden fields of scented Daffodils. Lines and lines of beautiful flowers. Sensuous, rumbustious golden flowers, embracing The wind as it gently sweeps them along. How Wonderful the flowers. The sun it shines brightly. Speckles of light when dawn does arrive. How Nature fills my heart with joy. Oh such beautiful Nature.

Astronomy speaks

Most beauteous the stars, astronomy speaks.
Heavens abide the twinkled dust. Eternities roll thy
Favoured tongue. Disenchanted arrows of petulance
Rear a cankered head, embarking a density of
Ignorance wherein celestial orbits rise and fall.
Piteous thy mind, where visions deem thy sight an
Erroneous intrusion. Seek thy setting sun and
Fleeting thy vision where glorious beams of light do
Descend from heavenly spheres, embracing solitude
And harmony forthwith and yet in persuasive eye do
Pry the substance of the soul. Wishing thy travels
Ascend to beyond thy visionary sight, to fields of
Stars and a rolling universe beyond thy mind.

Dream of past

When the meadows show a glazing dew and fields
Are full of sunlight, I give my thoughts to memories
Of past. Laid upon a grassy verge I bring forward
My past into the now. How the meadows green look
So sweet. Upon the hills are sheep that wander. How
I do love the quiet of day, as I lay and dream of past.

Winter woe

When winter comes in the cold dark night do I sit
Abandoning my heart. Thoughts of love that run
Through my inquiring mind, summoning great
Strength to pursue my judgement of past. Throw
Aside thoughts of unhappier times and relinquish a
Troubled soul. Finding cold, cold, comfort at the
Bottom of my glass. 'Tis time of winter woe.

Summer's day

I wander through fields kissed by a golden sun. I
Smell the breeze which captures nature beneath its
Wings. I ponder thoughts of days gone by, thoughts
Of me and you. I capture beauty in my vision and
Caress the gentle wind that tenderly nurtures and
Disguises its ill intent so well. I ask of thee O gentle
Sun to shine gloriously upon mine heart. I watch as
Daffodils like soldiers march together in triumphal
Mood, billowing back and forth. I count the hours
That day did bring and thoughts I ponder thus did
Say my, my, what heavenly day. Birds my friends
Whose songs delight, my ears are blest and thus my
Heart and `tis I who inquire did love ever capture
The essence of beauty so much, as my walk this
Summer's day.

Pleasure to seek

'Twas night falleth betwixt the heavenly sun and
Moon that deceived my eyes. For such beauty gone
In moments of time. Fade from view o glorious
Daylight and behold the magic of night, whereupon
My eyes fill with heavenly wonder. My patience `tis
Extraordinary to deliberate upon that which is
Beauty by day, and that which is beauty by night.
The sun rise and the sun doth set and stars, which
Fill the heavens gloriously, rise and fall. My vision
Filled and magic doth flow before me. For `tis
Through heaven's door I peep to then thus sleep, for
When my vision is done then wait for morrow to
Come and I more pleasure to seek.

Crocus bulbs and tansy fly

Crocus bulbs and tansy fly, cast the devil there to
Die. Butchers blade, carving maid, a search of life
Persuade. Magic night, silent moon, conducting
Music, symphonic sound, death in night of June.
Rain infested brook, a winter's tale, It must be said.
Cast thy secrets to the wind and seek thy soul within.
To die and leave this life when gone, all bright and
Sullen. To part this life on winter's day, reflected
Solitude and magnitude, pented frustration be. Maid
Of lust and child of hope and merriment after tea.
This to find my noble mind at work with words to
Play. In mind's eye my vision seen. To write is to
Orchestrate and together is to breathe.

Heavenly moon

Thou hast most beauteous eyes, a smile to tease and
Tempt, to please, yet pleasures seek beyond thy face
Of night. Oh moon thou hast such beauty,
Surrounded by opulent stars whom serenade thee,
Abundance of darkness your friend. Wherefore dost
Thou moon hide your silver tongue, whom whisper
To the sun and speak thy wisdom of the night? Pray
Tell me Insincere, but if thy beauty o moon did
Deceive and my patience thus did wane, nay more to
Seek the audacious moon and pleasure my eyes with
Such beauty. Wouldst thou speak unto me mere
Words of disdain? Yet methinks patience a friend
And I to wait for night to end. Oh beautiful moon,
Speaketh words unto me and I a slave to your vision.
What glorious sight thou truly art. Most heavenly,
Heavenly moon.

Magical night of stars that fall

Gaze amongst the fallen stars and take upon the
Courage to lift thy eyes to browse at nature's beauty.
Seek thy soul among clouds of white and lose thy
Mind in imagery not seen in light of day. Peep
Behind the sultry moon and see friends departed
Thus. Oh magical night of stars that fall from
Heavenly skies, pray upon thee do I and wish my
Dreams come true!

Hark thee oh bird

Hark thee oh bird. Oh bird whom sing, hark thee.
Dost thou sing a sweetened melody to please me,
This hour, this day? Does life hear your call, your
Beautiful song echoing gently on the breeze, that sail
So swiftly past? Hark thee well thy bird in flight, who
Arrows in the night beguiling the wisdom of the owl,
Whose tale she never tell. But hark thee well oh bird
Who fill the air with joyous tone. Hark thee well and
I can tell the whispered voice, the eye of night who
Howls a derivative crie and sigh. But well the bird
May lark and bark but sweetly pry into the night with
Voice. Oh heavenly voice to sing the soul to sleep.
But hark thee well and peace to mind I shall find. So
Hark thee well my friend.

The riverbank

I wander along the riverbank, the wind it blows but
Gentle. I seek to find the answers of my very
Existence. Oh for the flowers that grow. The petals
Fall upon the ground like patterns of silk in its flow.
I see such beautiful things of which they make me
Glow, such beauty to have to see along the river
Bank. Trusted friends, the birds feeding on the
Worms that are earthbound. Joyous sun, it does
Pound down upon my sweating brow. The grass it
Has such depth, it moves gently in the breeze. I see
Such colour from all around, the colour of the seeds.
How this does please my eyes, such beauty.

Appear unto me

Fallow or dale, brook or stream, howling river
Appear unto me. Appear unto me, so wild and so
Free, my fallow, dale, brook, river or stream

Oh to be a bird

Oh to be the bird that flies. Oh to be so free. Oh to
Be the bird that fly, so free, that's me. To feel the
Breeze. To fly with ease. Oh to be the bird so free.
Where dreams and aspirations lie where birds they
Fly so high. Oh to be a bird that's me. A bird so free,
So free that's me. Oh to be a bird.

Magic of night

When as day begins to slide, I gaze from out of my
Window to see shadows drifting into the night. The
Moon begins to appear against the silver lining of
The clouds. How when nature turns from day to
Night do I sit and gaze aghast at such creation.
Peering into ocean-less space, extracting acres in my
Vision, but understanding so very little. This is the
Magic of night.

Night of most beauteous sky

What dreams may cometh this hour, this night,
Where galaxies with pride do splay. Where stars do
Maketh such impressive sight, my eyes do ponder
Much, such is to say bountiful beauty my eyes do
Cast. Eternity beyond my wildest dreams. Forever to
Gaze and browse, may ever it last. Never a moment
Dull or sullen but infinite in its realms. Alchemy
Fused between a mind perplexed and inspired muse.
Thoughts do ponder thus elated I, a soul divine, for
This vision 'tis all mine. This vision that captivates
And intoxicates my existence. 'Tis my sight to spy
With eye this night of most beauteous sky.

The crested lark

Crested lark how you do sing so sweetly. A voice
That has no equal. You bring unto me the joyous
Tones that do set my heart afree. Crested lark sing
Your sweet song of joy that it may bring laughter in
The hearts of all. O crested lark please sing unto me!

Heavenly sun

Oh sun, I do look upon thee with great affection for
Thou art truly wondrous. My brow doth sweat from
Hard days toil but you lazily gaze down from
Heavens above, casting judgment upon me, laughing
Wickedly at thy daily deed. But sun thou art most
Beautiful and I speak fondly of thee. Wouldest thou
Sun change with me this day and do but my daily
Deed and allow of me a lazy day? Oh sun would you
As a God forgive my preposterous thought.
Perchance I dream too well but forgive me, for in
Honesty I speaketh unto you my friend. My dear
Friend oh heavenly sun.

Heaven's door

How the skies do speak unto me words
That ease expression. How the stars do rejoice in
Sweet voice and nature springs eternal glee. How
Heaven's door is before me, my vision implored.
A self satisfying illusion of night where the wishes
And dreams of the soul do thrive in emotional
Harmony at the sight of creative bliss. Share with me
The mesmerising quality before thee. Patience
Precludes wisdom and the mind fulfilled. Glorious
Substance of sun, sky and air. Frivolity proclaims
Me, wherein the moon doth raise a sober head to
Peep with eyes of deepened red and like majestical
Words 'tis said creation did ever send a visionary
Sight so glorious to eye and mind.

Papa Meilland

What rose can compare with your sweet fragrance?
If ever I did describe beauty in a scent, it would be in
The divine smell of the Papa Meilland

MIND

Silent whisper

Silent whisper thou voice unheard. Echoed vision of Silence. Persuade me silent voice, embark on me nay Choice. Oh whispered secrets doth tell, evolving my Spiral down. Embittered knowledge entrusted in Perpetual deviance. Stabled ferocity of hope. Forbade thy tongue that whisper silent words to Torment. A lover's harp to play thy tune. Missing Embrace of lover's twine. Ceremony of a foolish Swine. Decree the notion of hate, pitiful hate. Thus Oh me, and the Silent whisper.

I and me

I and me thus a twinning of incoherent harmony.
Imbalanced but defined, ready and sublime I and
Me. 'Twas nay a memory, a figure of eloquence seen,
But I and me a perfection of mind. 'Tis relevant I
Can see a description of I and me, as being a
Symphony of sweet music thus played. You see I
And me are mad, mad and sad but happy and glad.
'Tis I and me and my perfection of mind.

Divide of man and mind

What soothing conscience play its jest and yet what
Heart torn. So weary, so tired, this path of life's
Tedious travesty. O majestical matter that merely life
Could ponder its state of infinity. What persecuted
State render me inconsolable? Pursuing
Remorselessly a vision of heart, but tender be the
Mind when pity play this day. If I am to find
Happiness then frivolity allow of me pain to
Discover that which can ease my blame of this path
Of inconsequence. If but mortals play tell I may thy
Secret well and yet if thy mind could send its picture,
Wouldest thou see but empty illusions? Thus
Persuading ignorance and intolerance, along their
Way. May I suggest one may pretend that life, so
Long life, has mercy in its soul. But alas as fortunes
Sway from day to day memories becometh
Nightmares, toiled in shadows of ambiguous deceit.
For what is so long life? But to breathe, to see, to
Hear. Too long on life's earth sheltering in dishonest
Wealth of empty heart. For that which one must find
To learn of so long life, the soul, the spirit, the
Infinite divide of man and mind.

Upon a hill

Upon a hill I do sit, and ponder at such whims.
Leave me unto my dreams that I may drift upon my
Hill. Let my mind wander, so that it finds pleasure
Wherever it goes. Let the day drift from me, that
Night may come and I can rest. And unto my sleep
Let my soul be rested. But for now, just drift my
Mind into the unknown.

Yesterday's dream

Withered my beautiful memory. Were it spring when
Love did bloom? And yet my muse say winters fall.
Withered my memory. 'Twas summer's sun when I
Did hold thee in mine arms and yet 'tis memory
Betrayed, 'twere autumn turn. A beauteous maiden
Did pass my way, and the rose did ere before me
Bloom. Ah my memory gone, lost in time. A
Figment, an illusion seen and yet thou art a memory
That belong to past. My mind betray me. Beauty
Long in thought do please, but thou art lost in
Memories and yesterday's dream.

Conscience

Oh conscience be my guiding light. Art thou an
Illusion on this here night? Forbidden to speak for
Fear of offend, Oh conscience be my guide. To
Speak not doth make my anger rage, whence I
Imagine a gentleman's blade that cut thy conscience
Into two! Fear, anger, retorted view of degrading
Mind thus to find, thy conscience doth reside to
Which side? Art thou so hard to please conscience
Of which I heed your judgement?

Despairing conscience

My despairing conscience torn in two, finding
Irrelevance a sordid friend. Perpetual deviance,
Soiling a mind. Weakened, pitied am I to choose
Between a conscience soiled and truth. Pervade me a
Tolerance of dignity, pursuing a mind of
Indifference. Perceive in mind's eye a tolerant side, a
Conscience to trust, but woe is me. 'Tis time of
Madness. Melancholy me, and a conscience soiled.

The beauty of mind

Though blind my eyes and I no vision to see 'tis a
Beauty held deep in mind. A lover gone, yet beauty
Stay forever locked away. Beauties vision still has
First 'Twas taste. Perchance a muse to linger, O
Beautiful face. Heavenly bodies do delight. Celestial
Realms do dance in my imagination and glorify thy
Beauty. O for visionary sight, but where the eyes no
Longer bear witness, thy mind paint its extraordinary
Picture. If my wish thus fulfilled and beauty 'twas
Seen by eye, would ever it compare to the beauty of
Mind.

Conscience beyond repair

'Tis I whom aspire to the heavens above to dream of
Life and sweet, sweet love. Forbid my conscience a
Wasted space upon which to deliver such words,
Words, words, more words. To inspire, to delight,
The fickle and faint heart, of jester and of maiden
Fair. To dream of stars, moon and air thus
Persuading me of a conscience bare, empty like the
Fallen heart, a conscience beyond repair.

Beauty of mind

Beauty I do see compare to the autumn gone and the
Winter came. Thou beauty deep like the river bed
And fish they do swim 'tis said. For beauty untold,
Seen only by the eye of the beholder and I so blind
To all around, but thou beauty of which nature
Deemed a success. For thou art so rare and I so
Small, to see such beauty for my myself, captured
And chained in my vision. Pretentious I and the
Beauty I spy. For me, myself and I a beauty of mind.

The Astronomers mind

Maketh not my wisdom fail to thus seek of an
Infinite knowledge, where thy mind did seek forever.
Whence thy mind did race amongst fallen stars and
Planets beyond. To thus breathe a perplexing image
Of fantasy ending with heavens vision before me. O
Tell of my wisdom, O tell of my sincerity, that of
Which my visions do speak. Give to mind a picture
That doth send me in raptures of delight, to
Therefore hath my wisdom before me and given to
My soul a knowledge beyond my earthly existence.
To see heaven before me, like an open book that my
Mind doth read so well, pictures, images, one can
Tell. O mind race forth and heavens unfold. Stars
Glisten and moon be of proud state. And sun shine
Forth to delight my soul and give wisdom to me this
Day. For 'tis to say the astronomers mind doth play
And wander through fields of stars that dance, and
Planets who speak gloriously unto me. Such is my
Vision I now do see.

Mind and youth

Age decay, a beauty born, methinks my muse delay,
Yet in sweet persuasion my eye did see perfection.
'Twas not the delight of summer's sun when beast
And child do play. Perchance a heart, a burning
Heart, delivered a subtle phrase. Words thus
Breathed and I do say 'tis love. And through
Tormenting hours a suffering beyond my youth.
Methinks in twilight image, thoughts, a word, a
Subtle word and breathe I may my heart relay, the
Soothing sounds of love. 'Tis I and a madness
Beyond the mind. Perchance be I deceived and age
Decay the beauty of mind and Youth.

Poem on Dementia
The I Once Was

I sat looking at someone I knew I knew, but
Somehow I know them not. Each page of each day
Has lines that diminish one by one. You are not you
Anymore and I not I. I look in the mirror of time
And relate to so little. The I that I use to be is not
The I that I am now. All that is me is coiled in a
Spiraling oblivion of what used to be. My mind races
With thoughts of what I am to you. Expressions
Seem the only way you know, but know not, of what
I think, feel and am going through in my slow
Descent to death. Make me know, you know I know,
Touch me softly on the brow. Love will still be there
Long after the shell I become. For you, are you, and
I am me, individuals who once shared a laugh, a tear,
A cuddle. Now look at me, vacant, absent, no longer
There. Cry not for me, as I no longer need, my time
Has come, you must go on. Letting go is life's
Despair, so say goodbye to the I of now, but not to
The I once was.

WAR

The Poppy

The Poppy, a symbol of a human's greatest sacrifice.
They that give their life for a cause worthy or not.
Let it never be forgotten, that when the light goes
Out on life, if one has given it for that which they
Truly believe, the Poppy shall represent them. It is
The flower which grows where no one knows.
A symbol for mankind's eternal memory. You have
Not the beauty of the rose or the sweet smell of the
Lavender, but you will always be the only flower that
Cannot be forgotten. For those that have fallen are
In you!

Lost in the winds that blow

Though young am I and fortunes fade this hour, this
Day, I lay fallen with friends I barely know. Such is
This war, oh lovely war, where numbers not names
Have meaning. Dreams lay scattered in fields, with
Fires burning into the night. Wretched war, that
Cursed war, that scars the heart. Bemoan a soldier's
Life. A worthy man, but a worthless corpse in
Bloody fields far from home. Where is the reason?
Where is the hope? When letters to love one's
Penned, lay muddied, lost in the winds that blow.
War in anyone's name? Not mine or yours!

Weep for me (a plea from a dead soldier)

I tried for you, I cried for you and in the trenches I
Died for you. Oh England whom I love so well and
Whose life I shared but briefly. How I remember the
Sweet smell of lavender on the hill and the perfume
That you wore, my sweetness of home. I cannot
Leave the memory of the love I felt for that great
Country or the passion that stirred within my bones
For the dear, dear England. Become of me what you
Will in the blood splattered fields of death and
Despair, but I will fight till my last breath for you.
But who will weep for me as I lay frozen to the
Floor, with eyes open but pulse no more? Who will
Cry the tears for me, a soldier lost? I will dream of
Battles to come and for everything I have done to
Give to defend this great country, so far from me.
But hell, who will weep for me?

Land or riches

Friend or foe, enemy of woe, dredge my heart
Through the fields. Amongst the glory, amongst the
Dead are visions of lives that were led. Falling
Amongst the brave, crumbling in tears, these are the
Visions in the fields of death. War is here and I lay
Down to nightmares in both night and day. Spare
Me such turmoil, ease my broken mind, for war is
The evil which takes over men to die for nothing it
Seems. Visions of peace elude my mind and can only
Be in my dreams. A soldier's tale of woe is all this
Story is. Give the lives of men so brave not for land
Or riches.

If I were a soldier

If I were a soldier and cradled in my arms was a
Dying man, would I thank my lucky stars I was still
Alive? Or would I think for just that fleeting second
Of the child you once were, and the mother who
Held you like I do now? Would I then lay down my
Arms? Would I weep uncontrollably? Would I be
Half the man that I am now? I wonder if I were a
Soldier would I feel sympathy for that life lost? My
Enemy, my foe or perhaps my friend in another
Lifetime? Would I feel sorrow for those loved one's
You left behind? That last breath that you breathe,
And the thought that you have as life ebbs from you.
I want so much to be your friend now as you lay in
My arms. A soldier of war or just a man I never
Knew.

Could I do it?

Could I wave goodbye with tears in my eyes to
Family and friends, loved ones, children crying for
Their father? Could I stand as a man and walk away?
Slowly, painfully waving goodbye. And on the ship's
Bow from a distance could I see dear England as we
Sail away? Could I turn to the past and my memories
Many for comfort as slow away we pull. In leaving
These shores would the torment drag my mind to
The depths of despair, to wonder here and there
What is to come. Could I stand and fight for what is
Right with bayonet drawn on a foreign field where I
May fall and die, a death more painful than to say
Goodbye to one and all. Could I look in the eyes of
A man I know not and plunge in a thrust and a twist.
Could I see a man fall with death as my victory's
Reward? Will a photo fall from the fallen foe, a child,
A mother, a wife or lover? I don't know. Will I
Pretend my bravery as friends around me fall? Will
The fear that I have show through the uniform I
Proudly wear. Thoughts of 'you're a soldier do your
Duty, your country needs you' echo in my mind, my
Stomach knots, my throat is dry. Die a man you fool,
You think like a coward. I hear the distant blasts, the
Cries and moans, I see the wasted lives lay torn,
Soldiers scattered across fields where once flowers
Stood saluting the sun. Time ticks so slowly on hell's
Journey thinking of a return that may never come!

Soldier brave

War the song of the lonely. The dreams of the boy.
The bugle of the soldier played no more. War the
Thirsty man with the bitter tongue, the bite of
Poison to a good heart. Wear that pride ridden
Uniform, that rifle whose aim was true. For me a
Book to read, for them a misery. Down in the mud,
A frown on the brow, a contemplation of a
Home and a wife. Soldier, soldier where's the knife,
The blade to cut through life. The blood runs freely
On roads to hell. Death, oh death I smell. But what
Of the soldier a boy once was, with dreams? What
Dreams? A child now grown to horrible fate. I read
One more line and close the book able to enjoy my
Day. Tomorrow comes for me and the book that I
Read but for the soldier another day of hell awaits,
Awaiting death's door or the call to say the war is
Over. Come home soldier boy. Come home hero.
Think not so much of those you left behind, your
Friends, your enemies but freedom for your country
Made. Come home a hero, soldier brave.

Cemetery of war

Men, women and children. The brave and the
Scared. The worthy, the unworthy. The innocent, the
Weak, the fearless and the strong. The sacrifice of an
Empty cause. A calamitous judgment deemed fair.
Not even springs, rivers or streams can wash away
The thoughts of broken bodies, torn from life.
Sacrificial lambs to a slaughter. Someone's father,
Mother, brother, sister, son or daughter breathing
The air of this life no more. The weeping willow
Bears witness to such sombre mood. Cold and
Statuesque figures. Slabs of white, depicting a name.
How lucky you are to have a name. A monument to
A life once knew. Oh the savagery of it all. Mere
Segments of lives short span. A lifetime of memories
Dissipated into thin air. The soft, gentle breeze
Disturbs the sound of silence. Dreams abandoned.
Thoughts of tomorrow no more. No sun to brighten
Up this day, just images of horror etched in my mind
From a Cemetery of War.

Etched in some memory

Praying for this day to end as death surrounds me.
As scared as any man, yet I no more than a child.
Suffering each friend's demise as in horror I reel.
Sacrificing my sanity and all I once knew, little as That was.
Cold bodies, charred bodies, faceless Bodies abound.
Hearing the screams of fallen mates And those I know not.
Every sound I hear magnified in hell's tortured mind.
Nearing death oneself as shells descend. Good God!
Dreams, optimism, youth's filled hope, banished to nothing!
As pity rolls down my face in misshaped tears, pray for me won't you.
Every Soldier dreams a victorious End. If only!
Layed in mud, sacrificial lambs, butchered and slain.
Etched in some memory in Years to come, me and my fallen chums!

DEATH

Sleep like death

Wipe not your tears when cold death knocks, or fear
The loss of love once knew. Lay not the rose to
Wither on the grave, or watch the morning dew.
Hear not the birds come early morn, or count the
Hours but slow away. Hurt not inside for those that
Died, and grieve not to dismay. Time, life's short
Passage must there pass, like the memory of the
Looking glass, where pained expression seeks no
More. Rest your sweet and gentle head and off to
Sleep like death.

Here lay truth

Cold the body lay in the ground, no cares, no
Worries abound. Toils and regrets laid to rest, at
Peace the mortal beast. Death, the great bringer of
Dismay, the hands of time, fates cruel, cruel way. A
Flower cast towards the soil. The parting ways of
Love once knew, bound for heaven in sweet descent.
The earth becomes the mortal's joy. The stone that
Rests above the head is carved in tribute, three
Words are said HERE LAY TRUTH

My friend death

My friend death what doth thou tell as I slip from
Life a bitter hell. As my body cease to breathe nay
More, as sullen time did tick for sure. As through
Weary heart my soul did pry, as I lay forlorn about
To die. What maketh of my weary bones scattered
Beneath the earth's hard crust and a body once
Strong now turned to dust? Bitter my words as end
Is near, for where for art thou life to cheer? Nay
More to see a summer's day, as cold my body here
Do lay. For what is death that reality to pass when
My body breathes but its last? My soul departs and
Joy returns, for life begins at journeys end. What
Soul? What life? What journeys end? What hell
Awaits I know not now, as fear descends my
Sweating brow. A life too short to grieve, too long to
Deceive. No more tears I to shed. No more to
Waken from my bed. The time it ticks no more. No
Hours, no days, no more to laze for I am gone and
Dead.

One hour mine

Oh sweetest breath of a child's first day. Like the
Arrow from the bow, whose sway decides the death
Or life of foe. What is the life of one so small? To be
A man, so brave and tall. Who seeketh not of fame
Or friend, but maketh not the angel send. For who
Decides this wee child's fate, the hand of God? I ask
The stars who proudly dance, who doth make this
Child's first chance? To see, to feel, to play a role, a
Child of love? Of infinite woe? To speaketh loudly,
Oh so proudly this child my son, the devil's own.
Guess I speak the tongue of fool but who decides
Who I shall rule, the child, the slave, the gasping
Breath of crow? Look beside, above, below, the
Angels breath, the heart of woe. See the child in
Mother's arms, cradled, caressed, a love, a charm.
Patter little feet, ascend to God ye may, but not on
This your very first day. Be but mine an hour more,
See young child the open sore of love cutting blindly
The bowels of sin. Forgive my thoughts, oh joy
Within, oh love of child, but one hour mine. Love
Thee more than a blind man see. Who plays the
Fool? I shall not tell oh child who comes but one
Hour mine.

Death do tell

To die and sleep for endless time, my conscience
Thus depraved. No more to think, no more to value
Life's existence. A wasted sentiment, a single rose
Withered in time. Closed my door on sweet, sweet
Life. An empty vessel of which once I did sail proud.
Wallowing in pity my thoughts abandon me, cast
Upon the winds that blow. The sun doth shine half a
Smile and yet I know no return to these shores,
Where once trodden pained footsteps leave but their
Mark. Go forth do I to the land of memories once
Was. Left far behind a sweet, sweet life. 'Tis pain, 'tis
Suffering, the mind is forever embarking on a wasted
Voyage of yet to come. My friend death, do tell me.

The petals of a rose

To take the petals from the rose is to drain the life
From within the soul. To reach the smell of essence
Be, fragrance personified and still. Laid thus upon
The ground to seek the comfort of man's own
Existence. Harbouring on extortion he whom gather
Thoughts like seashells, so cheaply. Pragmatic fellow
Of no heart whom crie thyself to sleep at fear of
Death. The rose wither slowly in season's end, and
The pungent smell of sweet death gather momentum
And rain down upon the soul of sleep, drying the
Weeping eyes of one so empty. Dry the tears of
Sadness and whisper the soul to sleep, far beating
The drums of fate. Nay more to look upon the sultry
Rose, and gaze down upon the sweetness that ooze
Life. The trembling hours of life's eternity, facing
Death and what it may bring patience, solitude and
Everlasting sweetness.

Oh death

Death the great escape. Oh death the adventure
Unknown. 'Tis solitude I must agree, but death so
Final as to render this life no more than a dream
Thus was. I proclaim misery at such thought.
Thoughts of death that capture my deepest muse
And throw turmoil to the wind, whereby misery
Captivates my soul. To die, this thought, a perishable
Thought, that torment within the mind that serve me
Well, and yet torture me at times of peace. Depicting
A nonsense of folly to which the day of death draw
Its breath, and intoxicates my mind, poisoning me
And crushing resistance, bringing me woe. Alas my
Mind no longer strong to evade such thoughts.
Death by which there is no escape and of which
Death is a consequence of life.

Pillow of tears – Mourning a Mother – The Cockney Bard

Lay your sweet head down dear mother of mine.
Wipe your tears for the children you have left
Behind. Cuddle me in my dreams of night, hold me
Like a babe in arms. Love, what else is there when
Life's sweet breath alas is no more. The goodbyes
Have ceased, and the memory of time passing by like
A clock whose hands are still. I long to tell you now
How beautiful you are. I scream so loud but to a
Silence where I can hear the roses cry. When life
Ends we succumb to pain of which only a child for
Its mother weeps and mourns. Loss the unbearable
Loss. Forgive me for my ills in troubled times. For
Giving me life's first breath. I could never forget
You, how could I? How could anyone who knew
You? The pillow of tears is my one reminder of my
Great loss and heavens gain. I will see you when
Time for me stands still. I know I will. I say goodbye
For one last time. One last dance among the flowers
Of spring.

Printed in Great Britain
by Amazon